Into the Light

Into the Light

A Collection of Poetry

by

Lynda G. Bullerwell

Into the Light
Copyright © 2013 Lynda G. Bullerwell
All Rights Reserved

ISBN-13: 978-0615906195
ISBN-10: 0615906192

Published by Water Forest Press
PO Box 295, Stormville, NY 12582
WaterForestPress.com

Layout & Design by V.R. Valentine
Edited by P. Valentine

Cover Art © Petar Paunchev
Back cover author photo by Billy Mathis
http://www.themathisstudio.com/

Dedicated to my best friend, Eloy Olivarez who left this Earth on March 31, 1995.

He was the first to encourage me in my writing endeavors and is now my guardian angel.

To my husband, Tim who is my rock, my light, my laughter and my shoulder to cry on.

To our family who means everything to me and gives me the strength and love to make it through anything that life throws at me.

To the many friends and poets who have inspired and supported me in my writing and in life.

Lynda G. Bullerwell

"A poem begins as a lump in the throat, a sense of wrong, a homesickness, a lovesickness."
                    —Robert Frost

Poems

Poems

Lynda G. Bullerwell

3:00 AM Frame Of Mind

I wish I could word-play with reasons
why stars shine
only when you and I

are beneath them

or contemplate directions that fireflies take
to marry fantasy with what is real.

If we could take a leap
within some 3:00 am frame of mind
and end up in the same galaxy,

would you mind?

We could laugh like imaginary friends
until light awakens us

from the dream that met your hand in mine.

I saw a shadow in a painting
that fit your silhouette
so I sat and waited for a signature
of that artist in Paris
so we could somehow be connected

and then I saw a shooting star.

A Certain Symmetry

Grandpa always wanted me to play an instrument;

bought me a shiny new guitar
said I would be the life of the party
one day,

but I packed it away in the case,
music in my eyes,

and picked up a pen-

found a place my tears could hide
falling softly upon petals,
wildflowers growing around me

blooming between syllables.

I was never afraid of the rain
caressing my face
wind carrying my whispers;

these clandestine wishes
as kisses upon constellations.

Still a dreamer,

I blew dandelions every Spring
and danced in the flutter that followed.

There was a certain symmetry
between my fragile heart
and his coy, half-moon smile.

His gaze met my glimmer,
poetic spirits entwined

spilling love in gentle lyric.

After The Kiss

After his kiss goodbye,
flitter of sigh echoes
as tears fall upon ivory cheeks.

He proposes the premise,
on one knee,
of how we shall love
when we meet again,
tracing footsteps into tomorrow;

his promise, leaving hope
within a glimmering last glance
before he disappeared

with a subtle whisper
of three words upon his lips.

Although callow in receiving adoration
in return,

I knew fate when it fluttered in

grasping it by the wings;
this future fringed in flowered anticipation
of so many dreams yet to be answered;

doodling my name on a napkin, in calligraphy,
softly married with his.

An Echo in these Halls

We used to tiptoe through poetry,

holding hands,
and sigh at the pages.

I picked petals to slip in my pocket
to savor for later
like hidden treasures,

hanging on to your words
like stars I had caught
whispered

within a glimmering moment,

but emotions got in the way
and now there is something green,
but not the grass, for it is dying here.

Where is the flutter in your syllables
you left like feathers for me to find
as invitation to dance
in rhythm with your heart,

for all I see is gray

with wildflowers growing
through a crack in the sidewalk

as I search for metaphor in a dandelion.

Blushing Cardioids

If life were an equation,

and my journey a map
leading to a desired destiny,

then, I shall skip to a resting place,
gathering my own wildflowers,
carving our names

in weeping willows along the way.

Let's share kisses
between lines of poetry

because the two do mix;

syllables take shape
when gaze meets sway
and lashes flutter
to whispered rhyme

left in his love note

inspired by a perfumed pillow
long after I have gone away.

To be called a pearl
in a vast ocean
could have been my undoing

as my little red box of letters
is too big for the ribbon;

his eyes shall tell the rest of the story.

I hear the sounds of alliteration
in my sleep
as tomorrow's poem pleads

to be penned at 2:00 am.

By All But Sleepless Poets

I think Heaven
can hear my vowels

at 2:00 a.m. when breezes
beseech my voice;
this hour of mourning

when tears masquerade as rain
and screams spill, unheard

by all but sleepless poets.

Music makes love to senses
symbols clashing in clouds;
my mind keeping time

in flutter.
I dream in flowers;

petals blooming without seeds
and some say my garden
can be too sweet for consumption;
my pen leaking love

to anyone who will listen.

Some things never change
like little girls and wildflowers.

Sometimes in fertile moments,
I neglect prayer
forgetting ears can hear more than pain-

red candles unlit at dawn.

Clinging To Grace

On those days
when earthly things drain my spirit
and feelings spill like rainwater

into this gaping hole
where a heart once was,

I force the whispers out;
unsung psalms from a lethargic spirit
clinging to grace.

In this poetic hour,
syllables, tangled
with lumps in my throat;

nothing but a sigh to speak,

perhaps it is time to just listen
to love, to laughter,
to any little thing that matters
or mattered once
when moons were full
and tiny feet tiptoed into my arms
dancing all the pain away.

I have seen faces come and go
stealing pieces of tenderness

every time.

There is, however, one constant;
a light that burns in darkest hours
and I will crawl to the ends of the Earth

to feel the flame.

Dreamer with a Pen

Some said her dreams
were black and white

and never ending.

She swore he gazed into the same sunrise
every morning, her pillow cold;
echoes whispering love

through mountains, unsettled

and tears formed a river
where reflections met in song.

"Catch my sun", he called
in enchanting chime of bell
and she walked on steps

silhouette fading
as footsteps followed petal.

Some whispered in corners
of one who watched stars
and painted love with her pen

as they choked on reality.

See her pass you by now;
heart, softly held in his hands
glimmer in her eyes,

and borrow the sparkle

to shed some light
in that dark hole you call

reality.

Envious Sky

Velvet beginnings

fluttering softly;
whispers turned lullabies

with a tune you could learn to sigh to.

Some say romance
lives only in old movies
and novels

by authors named Danielle,

but, I beg to differ
as I watch him pass by
and catch a glimpse

of the glimmer of love

glowing
in my own reflection.

Angels appear
in many forms;

dancing a luminous game
of hide and seek
with willing hearts

in an envious sky
of constellations.

Enlightened

Grace of glimmering stars
found me you

amidst the darkness,
I can breathe
as light seeps in,
hope filling every emptiness;

promises woven into prayer,

for, floods
nor unfriendly fire
can fight the flickering glow

of fate.

Gravity

Years have ripened my senses

as heartbeats skip rope
with trembling responses
to his touch;

sighs best left for 2:00 am

when silence lets starlight in
and I lie oblivious to time;

lashes knowing only
the reach of his whisper
as syllables leave parched lips;

breaths surrendering
only to kiss.

How can one melt in December?

I blame that look
in his eyes

and a parking lot full of stars.

Footprints

On these nights
when words steal my sleep;
syllables fluttering in

like fireflies in waiting,

is there a chance
that a heart cannot hold
enough breath for poetic sentiment

when passion seems to flow
from every crevasse;
covering her canvas
with much more
than tomorrow's sweet, sweet muse?

With you,
I could run through wildflowers
until I am out of breath,
for, who is to say that winter
has to be a cold place;

love, a blooming spring;
vows mirrored in whispered prayer
as petals fall gracefully;

two sets of footprints in wet sand.

For Keeps

Should I ever miss a chance
with your lips between syllables;

to sigh upon whispers
when glances are almost too much
for my heart to handle,

remember,

my eyes that first Summer
flickers of adoration flowing
in new embers
sparked by your smile.

Keep
always, your fingers
entwined with mine

as footsteps find company
not in shadows,
but beside us; our dreams
stepping stones
to paths yet undiscovered.

Should you ever doubt
this flutter is for you alone,

remember,

we have loved before
and will again
in ways inconceivable

to all but lovers like us.

Halo

In the midst of misty eves,
I found a sparkle;

an artistic resemblance of an aura
upon sky's delicate canvas
beckoning lashes to flutter;

the tune of chords strummed
to a symphony known by no other name

than miracle.

There are soft echoes
beyond life's giggles
where we dare to dance
into the pitter patter of harp strings
within heart's intricate contours.

If you can bear the ache;

the loss of Spring
to the chill of Winter,

bare feet shall feel flowers
of purest petal
as love finds a resting place;

sun's radiant glow
riding upon your halo.

His Last Poem

He has grown tired

of tracing her silhouette
through sheer ivory curtains
as she bows her head
in pastel whispers
of the shadow cast
when the moon hides
behind clouds of silver lining

He no longer wonders
when seas shall calm
as sails weather the storm
of rose colored thoughts
or dreams of any color
dancing in his head

He lives in gray
looking over his shoulder
draped in illusion
and when you look in his eyes,
there is only emptiness.

When the song is over
and the needle skips,
not even words
can make his heart flutter anymore;
He, who spoke of love
in utter fascination
who tasted kisses wild
in his multi-colored imagination.

He, who knew the soul
of a woman
undressing her ivory skin
in restless anticipation,
those ears inhaling sounds
of joyful jazz
now, sleep in silence

Spinning his wheels
the carousel ride is over

as he writes his last poem.

Hypothetically Speaking

I borrowed words from a professor
and tucked a Webster's dictionary
in my back pocket
so I would be qualified to communicate

just in case
you give me the time of day.

My therapist asked me last week,
hypothetically speaking,
what I would do if you were ever to show up
at my door.

I paused and said;
"I don't know if I would open it,
but, he never would."

Funny thing is
I used to dream of a happy reunion.

There I was
on a stage receiving an illustrious award
and you were sitting in the crowd

beaming with pride.

Then I woke up one day,
looked around at my cozy home,
my family asleep in bed,
glanced up at pictures of my grandchildren

and started counting my blessings,
(not my money.)

After all these years seeking your approval,
all the times I have felt inferior,
suddenly, I just felt sorry

for you.

Rejection is a painful feeling
like the arrival of an unopened letter
marked "return to sender,"

but, do you know what is worse, Dad?

the feeling of loss, deep in your gut,
somewhere underneath
that three piece custom fitted suit,

beneath the layers of pretense,

there lies a memory
of the daughter that you never knew.

I Am Starting to Hate Red

I could paint the walls pastel
and spiral syllables
into a staircase of blue

for you,

but, there are days
when sunshine is not enough
and even rain has a scent
of unfinished sentences

waiting for worries
to stop spinning.

I am starting to hate red
and the way it turns flutter
into steady beats of loudness.

He said we could just turn it off
and then, he whispered.

It was lovely sounds of blue;

it was sunshine, rain, soft
clandestine constellations waltzing circles
around an envious half-moon;

shimmer dancing between lashes
of a goodnight kiss.

I Forgot About Bluebonnets

I forgot about bluebonnets

as wings carried my heart
to Colorado's peak of perfection.

I no longer had to imagine
that clouds were mountains
as white glazed beauty dawned
upon my summer sunrise.

I could live on air alone;

as breezes swing my tresses;
diamond moments tracing cheeks.

Somehow sky cries different there,
storms whisper a sense of calm
drowning out anguish in canyon melody.

I get homesick now
for a place I never lived,
but kissed once
on dreamy afternoons,

but, I forgot about bluebonnets

and twilight moments
when fireflies verse the constellations.

You have to love the place
where your poetry was born.
As a friend once said,

there is nothing like a Texas sky.

If Love is a Waltz

Hear this flutter;
my heart weeping silent tears
to a 2:00 morning moon;

arms reaching
for Heaven's shoulder;

my soft cloud to fall into.

Only in Autumn
do winds paint the color of hope
covering soil with whispers of faith

until December's blanket finds us
with lash filled wish for wonder,

but I am Spring
and will always be
when he holds my hand

as long as butterflies
let my footsteps follow in grace
and petal's velvet kisses
are jewels adorning my hair.

If love is a waltz,

may poetry
always be our music.

If Only to Melt

In bashful eyes
peeking through the keyhole
until voices were silenced,

poetry was born in my heart.

It was my fairytale
when life was too real-
writing rhymes, reflecting

a prettier picture of love.

Fingers intertwined
with incessant faith,
I found poetry in psalms

and we three formed a circle.

Through the years,

I painted my tears on life's canvas,
in splatters of liquid longing,
sharing in empathetic sentiment

fragments of my heart.

In my book of memoirs

there are no diamond clustered cameos
nor black tie events
held in my honor,

My poetry will not be studied
in literary books
or carved in tombstones

[between parenthesis.]

I will always be that dreamer

     d
  a
  n
   c
    i
     n
    g

continued

Lynda G. Bullerwell

in my field of flowers

picking daisies, plucking petals

"he loves me,
he loves me not"

just a simple poet
that fluttered through life
whispering syllables of love

if only to melt
a heart along the way.

In the Backdrop

I could be the flower
in the backdrop;
the umbrella he holds

over them for "the kiss".

There is a bench in the distance
lonely and cold

as if aching to be part
of this whirlwind romance;
this symphony of silhouettes

in black and white

when goodbyes on a rainy night
under a street lamp
brought a flood of tears

while credits rolled.

Into the Light

I always wanted my own garden

but the sun never shined
in our corner of the World
as I sipped starlight
that escaped through the cracks

and swam in syllables;
thoughts dancing in stanzas-
the only glimmer in these eyes;

weighted whispers
just waiting to spill
upon twilight's canvas;

my favorite quiet skies.

So I flew,

in one perfect moment
within those same stars

to nurture my spirit,
and my very own garden
watching petals bloom

like it's the first day of Spring.

Kaleidoscope

Can we pretend that we are young-
eyes just opening to beauty;
butterflies watching petals unfold

while dusk serenades sleepy sun;
dreams sauntering between stars,

pausing to pose for the moon?

If love could whisper
inviting spirits to intertwine,
romance could bloom in colors

like daffodils at dawn

like visions
through a kaleidoscope

where light fills every shadowed place.

Kissing the Ground

If I could only kiss

each blade of grass blown brown
and savor every drop of rain,

promising to sigh
when wind meets desert sand,
gathering feather to dream upon

when the day feels less than fortunate,

my body begging to embrace
treasures that came before me,
draping my spirit in insight
once called illusion.

To grasp only a fragment of majesty
from that mighty mountaintop

would bring me to my knees in shame
for lack of appreciation

for all of the little miracles.

Leaving Imprints
(for my children)

Reach for my hand
across fragile soil.

Step softly

through tears
joining hands and seasons
where time flies

and wind song sweeps up dreams

leaving us weary,
but smiling.

We choose which path to wander
when there are forks in the road,
or seeds to sow,

whisper my name

or strum chords of wishes
through silken notes.

Run through flowers, wild;
carve your message
in the sands,

leaving imprints;
tiny hands

of children gathering stars;

fireflies filling miles of sky
in collective sigh

jealous of your shimmer.
You are breaths of morning,
feathered promises shining down

from rain dance, flutter
come these miracles of mine.

Love Letter

Leave syllables on my pillow
when I wake
and your scent to hold me

when arms cannot reach
far enough

for winds to brush my face

with whispered kiss
too soft to capture.

Leave petals
when all the flowers have gone
from my hair

and I will dance them
into hearts

painting our best memories
upon sunsets of your dreams.

Awaken

each dawn with me
as golden flutter
leaves Spring thoughts

in every season.

You will never feel Winter
within the warmth

of my waiting smile.

Metamorphosis

You showed me sun
in perfect rays of ripple
upon my face,

sent me shadows
when I needed shelter;

swept me up
with only tickle of wave
to make me feel holy

again.

I used to think love
was something unclean
slipping away from glances,
questioning intent
with relief in escape

to remain childlike
for many seasons.

Fatherless, fragile bud,

you watched me unfold:
pink petals in bloom
twirling in reflection;

winged beauty in flight
but, I owe all this sparkle

to you.

My Jewels Are Not Diamonds

He sang to me
of forever;
of love and a pretty pearl
and since then, the glimmer
remains like blue-green coral
in waves of emotion
written on heart carved sand.

Pieces of my heart
are marked
with prints of tiny hands;
of paintings of stick figured love
entwined
under sunshine perfect skies;

melodies still dancing in our heads.

There are syllables
that I have owned since birth
fluttering as clandestine thoughts
like constellations trapped behind clouds
begging for a way to shine.

Faith has followed me in whispers,
picked me up in tear clad moments;
wildflowers, my pillow,
and nourished me with fragrance of hope
to bloom in every season.

There is scent of petals
upon these hands;
perfect buds to wish upon;
to hold when dreams come true

and when I must go,
leave me pink blossoms
to rest upon
and light upon my face

until we meet again.

Petals Wilt, Then Bloom

Pieces

of my life
falling into place

petals, scattered
now gathered
blooming bouquet

memories lost,
then found
in feather, floating
folded between pages

lashes fluttering
new dawn

love's sweet rose blush.

Trust slipped

like slivers of sand
though my fingers

and suddenly I was small
worlds away
from my heart

parched desert wings
thirsting, surviving only

on dreams.

He doesn't see

the lines when I smile
and there's a sparkle
where the worry was.

I passed a reflection
and saw a girl

beaming blush;
a rose blossoming
in gentle hues

~ dancing ~

continued

as shades of serenity
twinkled about her silhouette

I stepped back,
looked again
to my surprise

that starry-eyed girl
was me.

Misty Thoughts That Move

Captivated by fog,

she walks on tiptoes;
a beggar seeking solace
wishing stars into existence,

before dark.

She loves

wildflowers in tresses
tempting fate with prayer;

leads unbelievers of romance
to dance
in the moment.

he motions to follow;
footsteps trailing magic
in swirls of sand
for poets to swim in;

words with substance
to feed dreamers like us.

Poetic Pearl

I held seashells to my ear;
poetry was the pearl, whispered

wishing, always
upon the brightest star
after everyone else walked away

no one believed I saw it fall.

On honeysuckle mornings,
peeking through shades at sunshine
as grass tickled bare feet

Even then, the scent lured me

velvet petals plucked
between my fingers

"he loves me, he loves me not,
he loves me!"
and I left a trail of flowers;
wore a white lace table runner
for a veil.

Grandma cried;
made me kneel and pray
for wealth, knowledge

and taught me to be a lady.

So, I spoke softly, stepped gently
but, with a little sway
fond of my femininity.

Some of us were born romantics.

Poetry, Like Love

Shadows call out to me

when vulnerability seeps in
under my veil,

for, it knows well of my blank canvas.

If I could only pen petals
pulsating passion;
letting love color my imagination

anything but black,

but my words,
they follow breezes
and leave me here, dangling

-somewhere in between-

watching fireflies play
in clandestine corners
where constellations refuse to shine.

I could borrow brush
and beat old memories to death
to free my fingers;
rip out my heart
to find shreds of emotion
to feed fate's fancy,

but poetry, like love,

cannot be forced
or left gathering dust
beneath dried flowers
of a bride's maid bouquet.

It must be nurtured,
given room to bloom
flowing in perfect rhythm

to the shape of a heart.

Precious Cargo

Grandpa picked apples

shaking branches
as I watched them fall.

He had to step higher on the ladder
(I thought he could touch the sky)
to get the shiniest one

just for me.

There was a basket full.
Grandma reached for mine
but I held it tightly

on the way home;

precious cargo
from his hands to mine.

He watched me with a smile;
a gift cupped in small fingers

eating until my tummy hurt.

I miss him;
his laughter,
the gleam in his eye

I believe he is with me still
as I choose the shiniest one

and I still can't finish the whole thing.

Saturdays at the Five and Dime

I helped Grandma carry her bags;
her blue umbrella tucked under my arm,
from Motts, then Woolworth's

(the one downtown.)

We searched for thread, needles,
and a brand new red apple pin cushion,

just for me.

She bought Brach's candy
by the pound.

(Grandpa always loved butterscotch.)

I wanted to stop at the soda fountain,
but she said we would go home
and drink black cherry Kool-Aid.

I always think of her
when I am in the kitchen,

especially when I bake oatmeal cookies
from my own red and white checkered cookbook
adding a pinch of this
and a dash of that,

but, they never taste quite like hers.

Lynda G. Bullerwell

Scent of a Memory

I remember trains
and the sound they made on those nights
lying fearful of that last call

and as March winds near,
I can taste the pain

as my tresses sway;
a fool to think I could run away
from these roses, rekindling

the scent of your memory.

Fourteenth day of February
came and went.

Yes, it's still my favorite day.

I still see you standing here,
holding one white rose behind your back,
your eyes, smiling sunlight

and I fall to my knees
shaking my fist at the stars.
They lied
when they said time heals all wounds.

twelve years after
and my spirit still lies shattered,

your Valentine written on my heart.

September Song

Golden ribbons fall
as dreams flitter past.

Soft sounds of solace
fill the empty night
with glimmer

as stars twinkle
like a whispered lullaby
kissing sleeping lashes.

Twilight tiptoes into dawn;

dew glistening in petaled glory
as September breezes dance
and shades of auburn

flutter like love into waiting hearts.

Songs Unsung

Words flowing swiftly, sting
like daggers to the heart

and suddenly, I am no one-

wings unpinned,
wind whispers through my tresses
as I try to stop time

while we live within this smile.

Morning petals shadow peace
as dew drops wash away

songs better left unsung.

Something Real

I want poetry in the park
kisses between stanzas;
my lover's song

whispered under my chapeau.

One rose behind his back,
fingers intertwined
lifting love from his knees

all the way to my heart.

Warmth of his skin
against my face;
his woes subdued
within my nurturing spirit.

I want a lifetime
of romance;
our dreams in bubbles

cascading onto wet skin
and kissed awake.

I want Spring every day
when his eyes meet mine.
We don't need a candle

to flicker.

Speechless

Somewhere between his gaze,
the blue calm of Galiano,
softness of ivory petals
(that didn't fall far from the tree)
and the tickle of my own wings in flight,

I lost my pen.

I picked up remnants from another poet's memoirs,
tasted the envy within the scent of black ink,
and found emotion of expression,

but the tears wouldn't flow.

How can this beating,
this breathless vulnerability,
be subject to such a searing thing

as silence?

Sway of Willow

We never got to sway
together on that porch swing
or feel the breeze

that only country roads can stir.

Butterflies still dance
in my memories and I see you
in fireflies;
hear your voice feeding me syllables
to spill in poetry like this.

You are the passion
behind my smile;
the courage
that helped me hold your hand

when you took your last breath.

Someday, I will have that porch swing;
with each glimmer of summer
and shimmer of constellations upon my face,
I will feel you beside me

like the sway
of a weeping willow.

The Journey

Turn my pages gently,
for fragile is the heart that dwells within.

I will not allow superficial things
to cause me one more tear
or waste one moment

better spent gazing into his eyes.

My fingers could be picking daisies
watching his smile

as he pulls them from my hair

and we fall

into the sweetest garden
which is life

realizing it is not which path we choose
that truly matters in the end,
but the beauty

in every starry night,

the blessing of each sunrise
and the wonder

of the journey.

To Be This Close

I am wildflowers,
and you, the wind
that whispers,

soft, through tresses

where gentle fingers play
love songs

as if chords
of a violin's delicate strum;
each stroke,

a sweet sigh;

a remembrance
of petals that fell
in July,
of pearls hand sewn
on a veil,

dancing through storms
and all of the reasons
why I want you

in my space.

Upon a Wing and a Smile

Lady is a flower;
stem strengthened by life,

tresses, petal soft
flowing in gentle breezes
catching clandestine sparkle

of falling constellations.

Appearing almost fragile;
her scented skin glowing
as moon shines, faintly

jealous of her light.

She basks in the afterglow
of accomplishment

singing lullabies to sleepy eyes,
still unaware of the strength
hiding behind soft eyes;

love fluttering within every blink
of feathered lashes.

Unchained

Hitch me up
to a forever star,

for, love makes this life
worth never walking into the sunset
without your hand

in mine.

I kiss this shiny gold
at least once a day
just for good measure,

and wish

every night that it still shines
through tomorrow clouds.

I love this tapestry
behind our heads;
colors swirling from the tiffany-style light
flickering upon cozy walls

and the picture above the mantle
with ivory vows
whispered from your eyes,

but I could walk away

from the cosmetic beauty
into nothing but constellations
as long as your fingers
are wrapped around mine;

live on breaths of love alone
with just a promise
of your touch
when darkness comes.

Vows to Keep

Love his eyes shining
within yours;
his smile meant only for you
and the giggle from the tickle
of his fingers upon your cheek.

Don't forget the flowers
and the softness of petals

f
a
l
l
i
n
g

like the tears behind her veil,

or the warmth of sand
between your toes
as initials were carved;
two sets
inside a crooked heart.

Remember the stars
you wished upon,
the moon that shone the night you knew
and the mountain you knelt upon;

a glimmer of hope in your palm.

Hold her as she weeps,
hold her up when she falls,
and always,
always hold her hand.

Lynda G. Bullerwell

Waltz of Syllables

We cannot dance,
but you dip me anyway;

your colors mixing with mine;

our canvas,
never without soul

as laughter keeps us in step

when the waves are rough,
we twist and turn;
straddling ideas of hope

as trust is born
in eyes of lovers.

You give my heart tempo;
tresses swaying with hips

and every little thing
becomes a lyric;
each syllable,

a soft whisper of simile

you and I;
a metaphor for love,

and you said you couldn't dance.

Watching Butterflies Chasing Daisies

Poetry, like love
seeps into the skin
peeking into petals

when only a whisper will do.

Like breezes between tresses,
words wander

strumming strings of hearts
long thought turned to stone.

Yes, I do dare to awaken

flutters that lie
beneath faded smiles.

I traced his thoughts
as he watched a butterfly
chasing daisies

his unshaven face beaming,
eyes all aglow
beneath a golden sunrise
and it was then I realized

that we are never too old
for love

or poetry.

When it Lingers

I love goodbye kisses
in the morning;

scent of your cologne
lingering in the air,
brushed against my cheek

so I can miss you more.

I don't need pretty words
to know I hold your heart,
but, you whisper them anyway

just to see me sigh.

While Others Count Sheep

There are syllables flowing softly
between sheets
tickling my lashes to flutter

until I sigh
and climb out of my covers at 2:00 am

and let them out to dance

upon the keyboard
until I can breathe again

just about the time he comes looking
for his missing warmth
shaking his head with an understanding smile

because he is a poet too.

Some things just won't keep
until morning
like goodnight kisses that last,
a roaring fire

and words that whisper
from an unfinished poem.

Lynda G. Bullerwell

Acknowledgements

I would like to thank the following publications in which some of the following poems have appeared:

Skyline Review
Hudson View Poetry Digest
Epiphany Magazine
Write From Wrong Literary Magazine
On Viewless Wings Volume VI

Thanks to Billy Mathis photographer for Mathis Studios for creating the photo on the back cover.
http://www.themathisstudio.com/

Lynda G. Bullerwell

About The Author

Lynda G. Bullerwell resides in Texas with her husband, Tim and her Autistic son, Junior. She is also the proud Mother of two daughters, and 3 beautiful grandchildren. Lynda has been writing poetry for over 30 years and considers it her passion and a release for emotions since she was a child. Lynda has been published in literary magazines including Hudson View, Skyline Review, Epiphany Magazine, Writefromwrong and "Struggle" and has recently won first prize in Oneal Walters' 3rd Annual Women Inspirational Poetry Contest with her poem "Upon a Wing and A Smile".

The following pages contain reviews and praise for
Into the Light by Lynda G. Bullerwell

Lynda G. Bullerwell

A review of Lynda Bullerwell's "Into the Light"
By Jill Lapin-Zell

The reader is first struck by the poet's dedication, which is simple, eloquent and from the heart. And so are the poems that follow in this beautiful collection.

The poems here are wonderfully romantic and genuine. Poets over the ages have struggled to put that elusive essence of what it means to be in love into poetic form, but Lynda has come closer to doing so than anyone else I've seen.

Her poetry is soft and wistful and seems to float across the pages. This is no ordinary poetry.

In "Poetry, Like Love", Lynda tells us that "poetry, like love, cannot be forced or left gathering dust…It must be nurtured, given room to bloom flowing in perfect rhythm to the shape of a heart". And in "Blushing Cardioids", she suggests "Let's share kisses between lines of poetry because the two do mix". With these two pieces, as with the rest of the poems in this book, Lynda shows us that the lines between the feeling of being in love and the feelings that compel her to write such poems are blurred. We often cannot see where one ends and the other begins.

Lines such as "I knew fate when it fluttered in grasping it by the wings" ("After The Kiss") and "his gaze met my glimmer, poetic spirits entwined spilling love in gentle lyric" ("A Certain Symmetry") are only a few examples of the ethereal quality of Lynda's poetry.

A Review of Lynda Bullerwell's *Into the Light*,
by jacob erin-cilberto

"I wish I could word-play with reasons/ why stars shine/
only when you and I/
are beneath them"
says Lynda B., and if we allow ourselves to stand beneath
those stars, her poetry will shine upon us.

—————

"and then I saw a shooting star"
She is the shooting star and her poetry, the lingering spray
of words, as that shooting star crosses the sky.
And there is "A Certain Symmetry" to her work that is always
"blooming between syllables" bringing "clandestine wishes/
as kisses/ upon constellations." And Lynda is and always
will be "still a dreamer."
In this collection of poems she shares that dream of moving
"Into the Light"—and she is like her dreams, fluttering and
shimmering like the galaxy on a moon perfect night.
"We used to tiptoe through poetry/ holding hands/ and sigh
at the pages"
Lynda describes this event in "Echoes in these Halls"—
"I search for a metaphor in a dandelion" as this dreamer with
a pen shows us her dreams to be, not as "Some said her
dreams/ were black and white." But rather in spectacular
color—and "we borrow the sparkle" just for that too short
while as we read Lynda's poetry and hope it will "shed some
light" on our own "dark hole" we call "reality."—

Her reality is tender, loving—a way to "paint ourselves out of the pain of emotional abuse and abandonment and "Into the light."

We journey with this poet to "Colorado's peak of perfection" and to her home state where "there is nothing like a Texas sky" in "I forget about Bluebonnets," another lovely poem in this beautiful collection. But as Lynda says—"You have to love the place where your poetry was born."

And we are glad that she found that place and we readers love the poetry that was born there—

As she says in "Unchained,"

"Hitch me up,
to a forever star,
for love makes this life
worth never walking into the sunset
without your hand
in mine."

So unchain your mind, your vision, and let them walk hand in hand with this wonderful poet—

As you read this delightful collection of poems, you will fly to the sky of love and redemption and will not be disappointed. Instead you will return to this book over and over and soar into the mind of a poet who is as genuine as her work, and as beautiful a person as the one who shines through her poems.

jacob erin-cilberto (author of *Intersection Blues)*

Lynda G. Bullerwell

A Review of A review of Lynda Bullerwell's "Into the Light"
By Wanda Lea Brayton

Within these pages, you will find the wise thoughts of a person
who knows what it means to be fully human, who grasps the
fact that this life is all too brief as it is, who decides to make
the best of everything that comes her way. I am proud to call
her my friend and can assure you that she is, indeed, just as
strong and as real as they get ... a hopeful romantic in an age
that seems to discourage both.

     — Wanda Lea Brayton, author of *The Echo of What
Remains Collected Poems*